What to do When a Loved One Passes in California from an Eastern Orthodox Perspective

What to do When a Loved One Passes in California from an Eastern Orthodox Perspective

ANJELICA WOLFE

ISBN: 979-8-89228-047-1   (Paperback)
ISBN: 979-8-89228-046-4   (eBook)

Printed in the United States of America

CONTENTS

DEDICATION

I would like to dedicate this booklet to all pious and Orthodox Christians; my husband and high school sweetheart Stephen Wolfe and children Thomas and Chloë Wolfe. I would also like to thank, Dr. John Klentos; my vová (noná/ godmother) Dr. Ann Woods; Charleen Earley; Peter Tran; my parish Priest and spiritual family. I want to let you know that without your support and belief, this booklet would not have been possible. May God Bless you and have mercy on us all!

The Christ Pantocrator of St. Catherine's Monastery at Sinai, a 6th-century encaustic icon.
https://icons.pstgu.ru/icon/2036

STEP BY STEP GUIDE

1) Complete an Advance Healthcare Directive and ensure proper copies are given to Next-of-Kin. Find a funeral home/services needed/cemetery at this time.

2) When death is imminent, contact Priest to give Holy Communion before death and chant the Trisagion service after death (to be done at place of passing if possible).

3) Once a death occurs, Next-of-Kin must follow through with loved one's last wishes according to their Advanced Healthcare Directive.

4) Contact transport company or funeral home for pick-up (if needed).

5) Take time (do not rush) to find a funeral home (funeral director) that will help follow-through with the loved one's Advanced Healthcare Directive and religious needs. You may also go to the county of death for more assistance with paperwork, if needed.

6) Ensure Priest is included with the burial plans

INTRODUCTION

My name is Anjelica Wolfe, I am a funeral specialist in the state of California who converted to the Eastern Orthodox Christian faith in April of 2018. During my career of running a funeral home and being a part of Mortuary Affairs in the U.S. Army Reserve, I have served hundreds of families by helping them find peace and direction after the passing of their loved ones. In my years of experience, I have seen countless families taken advantage of in their time of need and I wish to change that by writing this informative booklet to help families prepare for and make informed decisions pertaining to the death of a loved one.

ADVANCED HEALTHCARE DIRECTIVES, WILLS, POWER OF ATTORNEY

CHAPTER 3. Custody, and Duty of Interment [7100 - 7117.1]
(Chapter 3 enacted by Stats. 1939, Ch. 60.)

7100.1

(a) A decedent, prior to death, may direct, in writing, the disposition of his or her remains and specify funeral goods and services to be provided. Unless there is a statement to the contrary that is signed and dated by the decedent, the directions may not be altered, changed, or otherwise amended in any material way, except as may be required by law, and shall be faithfully carried out upon his or her death, provided both of the following requirements are met: (1) the directions set forth clearly and completely the final wishes of the decedent in sufficient detail so as to preclude any material ambiguity with regard to the instructions; and, (2) arrangements for payment through trusts, insurance, commitments by others, or any other effective and binding means, have been made, so as to preclude the payment of any funds by the survivor or survivors of the deceased that might otherwise retain the right to control the disposition.

(b) In the event arrangements for only one of either the cost of interment or the cost of the funeral goods and services are made pursuant to this section, the remaining wishes of the decedent shall be carried out only to the extent that the decedent has sufficient assets to do so, unless the person or persons that otherwise have the right to control the disposition and arrange for funeral goods and services agree to assume the cost. All other provisions of the directions shall be carried out.

(c) If the directions are contained in a will, they shall be immediately carried out, regardless of the validity of the will in other respects or of the fact that the will may not be offered for or admitted to probate until a later date.

(Amended by Stats. 1998, Ch. 253, Sec. 2. Effective January 1, 1999.)

This is the most important document to have when a loved one is living, in fact everyone should have one. It is this document that survives after a loved one has passed. In this document, one can put their own wishes onto paper, such as life support, organ donation, what their religious preference is, what type of service they will have, and when they have to be buried etc. People can make these as precise or as ambiguous as they want, the more precise the better. If you want your wishes known and want them carried out, at least in CA, you need to have one of these filled out and given to your Priest, doctor, your spouse, and the hospital. Annotate whom you want to fulfill your last wishes, make sure to have back-ups in case the primary person passes before you or if they cannot be reached. This will help Funeral Directors, hospice nurses, the local parish, and other loved ones know who will be responsible for your disposition. Having these details clearly documented can save the surviving family members from some un-needed headaches. Make sure that the staples are not removed or altered, and that this document is only given to the aforementioned entities (Priest, spouse, doctor, hospital).

Wills

"A will is a legal document that states a <u>testator</u>'s wishes and instructions for managing and distributing their <u>estate</u> after death…" (Cornell Law School).

Wills are great when a person is still living, but this does not carry onward when a person passes away. Yes, it does state who will get what, but this does not account for anything with disposition of remains. I recommend that everyone should also have a will made and updated throughout their lifetime and ensure that the proper entities have a certified copy of this with no staples removed.

Power of Attorneys

"A power of attorney is a legal document that involves the agent or attorney-in-fact, and the principal. It is used in the event of a principal's temporary or permanent illness or disability, or when they can't sign necessary documents. The principal must choose a POA who they trust to handle their affairs for them. Documents can be obtained online or through a lawyer. Both parties must sign the paperwork. A third party is usually required to witness it" (Investopedia).

Power of Attorneys are an incredibly important document to have. POAs can be used to designate someone to handle your affairs after you pass which can help relieve a spouse of some unneeded stress. This document can also help prevent any in-family arguments since there will be no question as to who is responsible for disposition.

Summary of Advanced Healthcare Directives, Wills, Power of Attorney

These documents can be obtained and officiated via a lawyer or templates can be found and printed online. I highly recommend that everyone has these documents together and up to date as life goes on. Having these documents ready will make funeral arrangements and family discussions much easier.

NEXT-OF-KIN

The Next-of-Kin is the person who is responsible for signing all of the documents needed for the funeral service/disposition/payment, etc. The Next-of-Kin is the only one with whom the funeral director is legally allowed to discuss the disposition of the deceased. As mentioned previously, having an Advanced Healthcare Directive or a Power of Attorney, makes this process easier, by stating who will have the responsibility of disposition. Stated above is the law in California, this is what we follow and we cannot deviate from it. Simply stated, this is the order for the Next-of-Kin:

1. An agent with Power of Attorney
2. The competent surviving spouse (for example, spouses suffering from dementia are not competent and you will need a letter from a physician that states this).
3. Surviving competent adult child or children (example, if there are 5 children, you would need 3 to come to an agreement on arrangements).
4. Surviving competent parent or parents (there must be an effort to locate/get in contact with an absent parent before a single parent can sign off).
5. Surviving competent sibling or siblings (the majority and an effort must be taken to contact all siblings).
6. Surviving competent adult person or persons in the next degree of kinship.
7. A conservator of the person
8. A conservator of the estate

There are also reasons as to why someone who is in the order of succession shall not legally be the Next-of-Kin as stated below in the Health and Safety Code 7100.

CHAPTER 3. Custody, and Duty of Interment [7100 - 7117.1]
(Chapter 3 enacted by Stats. 1939, Ch. 60.)

7100.

(a) The right to control the disposition of the remains of a deceased person, the location and conditions of interment, and arrangements for funeral goods and services to be provided, unless other directions have been given by the decedent pursuant to Section 7100.1, vests in, and the duty of disposition and the liability for the reasonable cost of disposition of the remains devolves upon, the following in the order named:

(1) An agent under a power of attorney for health care who has the right and duty of disposition under Division 4.7 (commencing with Section 4600) of the Probate Code, except that the agent is liable for the costs of disposition only in either of the following cases:

(A) Where the agent makes a specific agreement to pay the costs of disposition.

(B) Where, in the absence of a specific agreement, the agent makes decisions concerning disposition that incur costs, in which case the agent is liable only for the reasonable costs incurred as a result of the agent's decisions, to the extent that the decedent's estate or other appropriate fund is insufficient.

(2) The competent surviving spouse.

(3) The sole surviving competent adult child of the decedent or, if there is more than one competent adult child of the decedent, the majority of the surviving competent adult children. However, less than the majority of the surviving competent adult children shall be vested with the rights and duties of this

section if they have used reasonable efforts to notify all other surviving competent adult children of their instructions and are not aware of any opposition to those instructions by the majority of all surviving competent adult children.

(4) The surviving competent parent or parents of the decedent. If one of the surviving competent parents is absent, the remaining competent parent shall be vested with the rights and duties of this section after reasonable efforts have been unsuccessful in locating the absent surviving competent parent.

(5) The sole surviving competent adult sibling of the decedent or, if there is more than one surviving competent adult sibling of the decedent, the majority of the surviving competent adult siblings. However, less than the majority of the surviving competent adult siblings shall be vested with the rights and duties of this section if they have used reasonable efforts to notify all other surviving competent adult siblings of their instructions and are not aware of any opposition to those instructions by the majority of all surviving competent adult siblings.

(6) The surviving competent adult person or persons respectively in the next degrees of kinship or, if there is more than one surviving competent adult person of the same degree of kinship, the majority of those persons. Less than the majority of surviving competent adult persons of the same degree of kinship shall be vested with the rights and duties of this section if those persons have used reasonable efforts to notify all other surviving competent adult persons of the same degree of kinship of their instructions and are not aware of any opposition to those instructions by the majority of all surviving competent adult persons of the same degree of kinship.

(7) A conservator of the person appointed under Part 3 (commencing with Section 1800) of Division 4 of the Probate Code when the decedent has sufficient assets.

(8) A conservator of the estate appointed under Part 3 (commencing with Section 1800) of Division 4 of the Probate Code when the decedent has sufficient assets.

(9) The public administrator when the deceased has sufficient assets.

(b) (1) If a person to whom the right of control has vested pursuant to subdivision (a) has been charged with first- or second-degree murder or voluntary manslaughter in connection with the decedent's death and those charges are known to the funeral director or cemetery authority, the right of control is relinquished and passed on to the next of kin in accordance with subdivision (a).

(2) If the charges against the person are dropped, or if the person is acquitted of the charges, the right of control is returned to the person.

(3) Notwithstanding this subdivision, no person who has been charged with first- or second-degree murder or voluntary manslaughter in connection with the decedent's death to whom the right of control has not been returned pursuant to paragraph (2) shall have any right to control disposition pursuant to subdivision (a) which shall be applied, to the extent the funeral director or cemetery authority know about the charges, as if that person did not exist.

(c) A funeral director or cemetery authority shall have complete authority to control the disposition of the remains and to proceed under this chapter to recover usual and customary charges for the disposition when both of the following apply:

(1) Either of the following applies:

(A) The funeral director or cemetery authority has knowledge that none of the persons described in paragraphs (1) to (8), inclusive, of subdivision (a) exists.

(B) None of the persons described in paragraphs (1) to (8), inclusive, of subdivision (a) can be found after reasonable inquiry, or contacted by reasonable means.

(2) The public administrator fails to assume responsibility for disposition of the remains within seven days after having been given written notice of the facts. Written notice may be delivered by hand, United States mail, facsimile transmission, or telegraph.

(d) The liability for the reasonable cost of final disposition devolves jointly and severally upon all kin of the decedent in the same degree of kinship and upon the estate of the decedent. However, if a person accepts the gift of an entire body under subdivision (a) of Section 7155.5, that person, subject to the terms of the gift, shall be liable for the reasonable cost of final disposition of the decedent.

(e) This section shall be administered and construed to the end that the expressed instructions of the decedent or the person entitled to control the disposition shall be faithfully and promptly performed.

(f) A funeral director or cemetery authority shall not be liable to any person or persons for carrying out the instructions of the decedent or the person entitled to control the disposition.

(g) For purposes of this section, "adult" means an individual who has attained 18 years of age, "child" means a natural or adopted child of the decedent, and "competent" means an individual who has not been declared incompetent by a court of law or who has been declared competent by a court of law following a declaration of incompetence.

(h) (1) For the purpose of paragraph (1) of subdivision (a), the designation of a person authorized to direct disposition (PADD) on a United States Department of Defense Record of Emergency Data, DD Form 93, as that form exists on December 31, 2011, or its successor form, shall take first priority and be used to establish an agent who has the right and duty of disposition for a decedent who died while on duty in any branch or component of the Armed Forces of the United States, as defined by Section 1481 of Title 10 of the United States Code.

(2) This subdivision shall become operative only if the United States Department of Defense Record of Emergency Data, DD Form 93, and Section 1482(c) of Title 10 of the United States Code are amended to allow a service member to designate any person, regardless of the relationship of the designee to the decedent, as the agent who has the right of disposition of a service member's remains.

(Amended by Stats. 2011, Ch. 321, Sec. 1.5. (AB 905) Effective January 1, 2012.)

PRENEEDS VS. AT-NEEDS

"Preneed arrangement," "preneed agreement" or "preneed" is written instruction regarding goods or services or both goods and services for final disposition of human remains when the goods or services are not provided until the time of death, and may be either unfunded or paid for in advance of need.
Cal. Code Regs. Tit. 16, § 1277

Preneeds are arrangements that are made and paid for before someone passes away. This is another option for people who want to make sure that their family does not have to worry about anything in regards to disposition. Be sure that your Next-of-Kin has a copy of these documents, if they do not, you would just be wasting your time and money. For example, if you pre-paid for services (a Preneed) and you do not inform the Next-of-Kin, then those services and monies spent will not be reimbursed or used. Even though you have prepaid for certain services, there will still be additional fees for services rendered such as death certificates and transportation. Ensure that everything you want is written in full detail, signed, and copied.

ARTICLE 9. Preneed Funeral Arrangements [7735 - 7746]
(Article 9 added by Stats. 1965, Ch. 1414.)

7745.

Every funeral establishment shall present to the survivor of the deceased who is handling the funeral arrangements or the responsible party a copy of any preneed agreement which has been signed and paid for in full, or in part by, or on behalf of the deceased and is in the possession of the funeral establishment. The copy may be presented in person, by certified mail, or by facsimile transmission, as agreed upon by the survivor of the deceased or the responsible party. A funeral establishment that knowingly fails to present a preneed agreement to the survivor of the deceased or the responsible party shall be liable for a civil fine equal to three times the cost of the preneed agreement, or one thousand dollars ($1,000), whichever is greater.

(Amended by Stats. 1996, Ch. 1151, Sec. 47. Effective January 1, 1997.)

Also note, that you must receive a copy of the preneed agreement while contacting the funeral home to fulfill the preneed. This is to ensure that the funeral home and the Next-of-Kin have a mutual understanding of what exactly the preneed states and what it does and does not cover.

"At-need" means at the time of death or while death is imminent (Law Insider).

An at-need is when you purchase your funeral services at or shortly before the time your loved one passes away. This is an option for people who have an Advanced Healthcare Directive in place and their Next-of-Kin are well aware of what their last wishes are. People who have an unexpected death are also under the at-need category. Do not call a funeral home while under duress or cloudy thinking, the reasoning for this is simple. When someone is under duress and completely lost in a sense that they lost a loved one, the mind is sometimes not able to fully comprehend full contracts or services. Which can sometimes lead to family members or friends being taken advantage of, due to "wanting to get it over with." "Grief and loss affect the brain and body in many different ways. They can cause changes in memory, behavior, sleep, and body function, affecting the immune system as well as the heart. It can also lead to cognitive effects, such as brain fog" (https://www.americanbrainfoundation.org). The Next-of-Kin does have the authority to assign someone to reach out for funeral arrangements at this time, but this does not negate their responsibility of disposition. For example, when my grandmother passed away, my father had me reach out to different entities on his behalf due to his grief, but he was still responsible for signing paperwork and paying for services.

PASSING AWAY AT HOME

If passing is imminent, contact your parish Priest to see the loved one. Sometimes people will not be in a state to fully receive Holy Communion (i.e. unconscious). This is where the Priest will be able to console and help the family with the next steps for the loved one. Such as prayers, confession, or if able Holy Communion. Orthodox Christians do not believe in Last Rites, that is a Catholic Christian understanding and practice. If the loved one passes away at home and away from medical assistance (such as hospice nurses, etc.), the family must contact the coroner to report the death. Once the coroner has determined the type of passing, it will be up to them to release the loved one back into the family's care or if the loved one must be taken to the coroner's office for further investigation.

Orthodox Christians follow certain precautions when it comes to autopsies, "Unless there is a specific legal reason, such as determining the cause of death, an autopsy ought to be avoided. The desire for scientific information through experimentation is not enough reason to merit an autopsy. Nevertheless, this is a decision that the family itself must make. The Church is concerned that respect for the body as the temple of the Holy Spirit be maintained"(*"Guidelines for Christian Burial", SS. Peter and Paul Orthodox Church, Manville, NJ*). Again, please rely on your Priest for further guidance if there is any confusion.

Once the loved one has been released back to the family (if still at home), the next steps would be for the family to decide if they would like to prepare their loved one themselves for viewing at the home or if they would like to contact a funeral home right then and there. Remember, if a loved one passes away at night, some transportation companies/funeral homes may have higher fees.

I have included the laws for the coroner to provide guidance on what to do, in case a loved one passes away at home and the family or Next-of-Kin does not have support or professional help available at the time of passing.

ARTICLE 3. Responsibility of Coroner [102850 - 102870]
(Article 3 added by Stats. 1995, Ch. 415, Sec. 4.)

102850.
A physician and surgeon, physician assistant, funeral director, or other person shall immediately notify the coroner when he or she has knowledge of a death that occurred or has charge of a body in which death occurred under any of the following circumstances:

(a) Without medical attendance.
(b) During the continued absence of the attending physician and surgeon.
(c) Where the attending physician and surgeon or the physician assistant is unable to state the cause of death.
(d) Where suicide is suspected.
(e) Following an injury or an accident.
(f) Under circumstances as to afford a reasonable ground to suspect that the death was caused by the criminal act of another.

Any person who does not notify the coroner as required by this section is guilty of a misdemeanor.
(Added by Stats. 1995, Ch. 415, Sec. 4. Effective January 1, 1996.)

102855.

The coroner whose duty it is to investigate such deaths shall ascertain as many as possible of the facts required by this chapter.
(Added by Stats. 1995, Ch. 415, Sec. 4. Effective January 1, 1996.)

102860.

The coroner shall state on the certificate of death the disease or condition directly leading to death, antecedent causes, other significant conditions contributing to death and other medical and health section data as may be required on the certificate, and the hour and day on which death occurred. The coroner shall specifically indicate the existence of any cancer, as defined in subdivision (e) of Section 103885, of which he or she has actual knowledge.
The coroner shall within three days after examining the body deliver the death certificate to the attending funeral director.
(Added by Stats. 1995, Ch. 415, Sec. 4. Effective January 1, 1996.)

102865.

In any case involving an infant under the age of one year where the gross autopsy results in a presumed diagnosis of sudden infant death syndrome, the coroner shall, within 24 hours of the gross autopsy, notify the local health officer, as defined in Section 123740.
(Added by Stats. 1995, Ch. 415, Sec. 4. Effective January 1, 1996.)

PASSING AWAY AT A HOSPITAL OR HOSPICE

When a loved one passes away at a hospital or a hospice center (or hospice care) you do not need to contact the coroner yourself due to the loved one passing under medical care/ surveillance. If your loved one passes at a hospital, they will give you a few moments to grieve (this differs from hospital to hospital due to different policies in place) and inform you to make arrangements or to see if the loved one has a preneed arrangement in place. The loved one will be moved to the hospital morgue. When a loved one passes during hospice care at home, the hospice care nurse will contact the coroner themselves to report the passing.

When you (the family/Next-of-Kin) have made arrangements for pick up and the funeral, a vehicle will be dispatched and the loved one will be taken to the storage facility/funeral home/ or the loved one's residence of the family's/Next-of-Kin's choice. Both hospitals and hospice may have their own forms and authorizations for you to sign in order to release or pick up.

During this time, please ensure that you know what the loved one's wishes were and to carry them out to the best of your ability as stated in California's Health and Safety Code 7100.

Often, funeral homes will have statements that might manipulate a grieving individual, such as, "…we will bring him into our care…" to trick families into thinking their loved ones will be stored in some barbaric way if they are not being "taken care of," this is far from the truth. At the hospital, they have larger refrigerators and in most cases have more room for your loved one then at a funeral home where their refrigerators look like a normal deep freezer. Please be aware of this and try to think as clearly as possible during these times.

TRANSPORTATION

Transportation costs should be put into a person's burial plan ahead of a passing (in the preneed) and should be an expected expense. Transportation is normally only mentioned during a first-call (right away when someone passes). Orthodox Christians have the Trisagion service, the funeral service, and the burial service. Transportation costs can range anywhere from $350.00 or more per one way. If we add pick up and transportation to church then to the cemetery, this could be well over $1,050 alone, depending on who you use for transportation.

For the Trisagion service, plan to have this done at the place of passing if possible to save on the transportation costs. For the funeral service and the burial service, this would count as two trips. When planning for these services, ensure that you confirm if you will be charged for each trip or round trip. This is imperative not only for budgeting, but for piece of mind for the Next-of-Kin.

This is an expense that is not always attainable for the average family. Families do not always need to hire for this service, since they can transport their loved one by themselves, if you have a van or large enough vehicle. If this is not something a family would like to take on, please check with your local parish or Priest to see if there is anyone in the parish that offers such services at a modest cost. This is why being involved within your church community is so important, even when you do not need help with a certain life event at the moment, you may eventually need to reach out to other brothers and sisters in Christ for help.

FUNERAL DIRECTOR SERVICES

Funeral director services/service fee is a fee that you must pay when contracting with a funeral home. Is this a necessary expense? Yes, the funeral director is responsible for death certificate/permit filing, funeral arrangements, logistics of transportation for loved ones (to and from place of passing, funeral home, etc.), ceremony preparation depending on last wishes/religious traditions, etc. Depending on how small the funeral home is, the funeral director may be in charge of the funeral home and all that entails.

Funeral directors are not lawyers, but they can help guide individuals with preneed arrangements and ensure those families adhere to California State Law. If you are uncomfortable or feel like you are being pressured into services that you do not want or that you cannot afford, feel free to tell that funeral director; if they still persist, find another one to work with. This is a professional career and funeral directors are held to a high standard of conduct and approachability, please have open communication and elaborate on what exactly you want and the funeral director should do their best to help.

ARTICLE 2. Funeral Establishments and Directors [7615 - 7636]
(Heading of Article 2 amended by Stats. 1998, Ch. 970, Sec. 31.)

7615.

A funeral director is a person engaged in or conducting, or holding himself or herself out as engaged in any of the following:

(a) Preparing for the transportation or burial or disposal, or directing and supervising for transportation or burial or disposal of human remains.
(b) Maintaining an establishment for the preparation for the transportation or disposition or for the care of human remains.
(c) Using, in connection with his or her name, the words "funeral director," or "undertaker," or "mortician," or any other title implying that he or she is engaged as a funeral director.

(Amended by Stats. 1996, Ch. 1151, Sec. 1. Effective January 1, 1997.)

DEATH CERTIFICATE AND PERMIT FILING

In order for a loved one's burial plans to occur, the death certificate and permit need to be filed and completed in the computer system EDRS (Electronic Death Registration System). This system is administered by the California Office of Vital Records. This normally takes approximately 2-3 days, sometimes more depending on the cause/circumstances around the passing. For example, if someone's death is unexpected and a coroner's case, this will postpone the official cause of death on the death certificate, and the coroner will put a holder line in the cause of death such as "...pending..." This will cause a delay and the family will need to stay in contact with the coroner. Even if a family goes through a funeral home, the funeral home will have to continually ask for updates on the case; please be understanding of that. The last attending physician can also postpone a death certificate from being completed quickly. Depending on where/how the loved one dies has a lot to do with the type of last attending physician, for example, if a loved was last seen by a surgeon, that surgeon might be busy and in between surgies and may not have the time to get right on the death certificate. Legally in California, the last attending physician must sign the death certificate within 15 hours after death and the county coroner within 3 days after examination.

ARTICLE 1. Duty of Registering Death [102775 - 102805]
(Article 1 added by Stats. 1995, Ch. 415, Sec. 4.)

102780. A funeral director, or person acting in lieu thereof, shall prepare the certificate and register it with the local registrar.
(Added by Stats. 1995, Ch. 415, Sec. 4. Effective January 1, 1996.)

102795. The medical and health section data and the time of death shall be completed and attested to by the physician and surgeon last in attendance, or in the case of a patient in a skilled nursing or intermediate care facility at the time of death, by the physician and surgeon last in attendance or by a licensed physician assistant under the supervision of the physician and surgeon last in attendance if the physician and surgeon or licensed physician assistant is legally authorized to certify and attest to these facts, and if the physician assistant has visited the patient within 72 hours of the patient's death. In the event the licensed physician assistant certifies the medical and health section data and the time of death, then the physician assistant shall also provide on the document the name of the last attending physician and surgeon and provide the coroner with a copy of the certificate of death. However, the medical health section data and the time of death shall be completed and attested to by the coroner in those cases in which he or she is required to complete the medical and health section data and certify and attest to these facts.
(Added by Stats. 1995, Ch. 415, Sec. 4. Effective January 1, 1996.)

102800. The medical and health section data and the physician's or coroner's certification shall be completed by the attending physician within 15 hours after the death, or by the coroner within three days after examination of the body. The physician shall within 15 hours after the death deposit the certificate at the place of death, or deliver it to the attending funeral director at his or her place of business or at the office of the physician.
(Added by Stats. 1995, Ch. 415, Sec. 4. Effective January 1, 1996.)

CHAPTER 8. Permits for Disposition of Human Remains [103050 - 103105]

(Chapter 8 added by Stats. 1995, Ch. 415, Sec. 4.)

103055.

(a) If the certificate of death is properly executed and complete, the local registrar of births and deaths shall issue a permit for disposition that, in all cases, shall specify any one of the following:

(1) The name of the cemetery where the remains shall be interred.

(2) Burial at sea as provided in Section 7117.

(3) The address or description of the place where remains shall be buried or scattered.

(4) The address of the location where the cremated remains or hydrolyzed human remains will be kept, as provided in Section 7054.6, under the conditions the state registrar may approve, including, but not limited to, conditions in keeping with public sensibilities, applicable laws, and reasonable assurances that the disposition will be carried out in accordance with the prescribed conditions and will not constitute a private or public nuisance.

(b) Notwithstanding any other provisions of this part relative to issuance of a permit for disposition, whenever the death occurred from a disease declared by the state department to be infectious, contagious, or communicable and dangerous to the public health, a permit for the disposition of the body shall not be issued by the local registrar, except under those conditions as may be prescribed by the state department and local health officers.

(c) This section shall remain in effect only until January 1, 2027, and as of that date is repealed.

(Amended by Stats. 2022, Ch. 399, Sec. 46. (AB 351) Effective January 1, 2023. Repealed as of January 1, 2027, by its own provisions. See later operative version added by Sec. 47 of Stats. 2022, Ch. 399.)

PACKAGES VS. À LA CARTE

When people think of funerals they think big expenses and thousands of dollars that need to be spent. Some people may hold off on arrangements or worse, abandon their loved ones at a funeral home once the cost is discovered. There is a federal law called the Funeral Rule law that protects people from being taken advantage of by funeral homes. You do NOT have to buy packages. State law requires that a funeral home must have a general price list (GPL) stating all individual costs. The consumer has the right to pick and choose services they want rendered. Most funeral homes abide by this rule. The only service the consumer cannot opt out of, is the funeral director services. As stated in a previous topic, you must pay for this service since, without the funeral director of the funeral home, no services/arrangements could be made, unless the Next-of-Kin make all the arrangements by themselves without a funeral home.

Here is the Federal Funeral Rule and where to find it:

"Under the FTC's Funeral Rule, consumers have the right to get a general price list from a funeral provider when they ask about funeral arrangements. They also have the right to choose the funeral goods and services they want (with some exceptions), and funeral providers must state this right on the general price list. If state or local law requires purchase of any particular item, the funeral provider must disclose it on the price list, with a reference to the specific law. The funeral provider may not refuse, or charge a fee, to handle a casket bought elsewhere, and a provider offering cremations must make alternative containers available. The FTC conducts undercover inspections every year to make sure that funeral homes are complying with the agency's Funeral Rule. The Funeral Rule applies anytime a consumer seeks information from a funeral provider, whether the consumer is asking about preneed or at-need arrangements." https://www.ftc.gov/news-events/topics/truth-advertising/funeral-rule

EMBALMING OR REFRIGERATION?

When it comes to the discussion on whether or not to embalm our loved ones, it comes down to what the family wants.

Embalming became widespread during the American Civil War, with families wanting their loved ones sent back home for burial. Embalming is a method that replaces bodily fluids with preservatives, such as formaldehyde. During embalming, the body is also prepared for viewing/burial, it will be washed, jaw closed, eyes closed, etc. Embalming is a more expensive option compared to refrigeration, due to the cost of the embalmer, supplies, and storage time.

In today's world, wonderful advancements in technology and great refrigeration are available for all loved ones. Refrigeration has replaced the true need for embalming during normal circumstances. Refrigeration is the most commonly used method to preserve a loved one until burial. This is the most cost effective and least invasive method. A loved one can be safely out of refrigeration up to 24hours, after this time it is highly recommended to place them back into refrigeration or burial immediately. Remember, some locations may have their own rules about this time frame as well, such as only 2 hours out of refrigeration. If you are planning to fly your loved one to another state or long distance (outside a refrigerator longer than 24hours) then you will need to place your loved one in a metal airtight container for transport.

In the state of California, you do not have to embalm your loved one. It is illegal for a funeral director or embalmer to tell you that your loved one must be embalmed. It is a choice and should not be pressured. There are some locations that require embalming and they are allowed to have their own protocols in place. If you choose not to embalm your loved one and are using a location that requires embalming, find another location.

This is a family's choice on which method to use, unless the loved one had made known of which option they'd prefer, there should be no pressure or guilt for using either method.

ARTICLE 1. Embalming [7300 - 7304]
(Article 1 enacted by Stats. 1939, Ch. 60.)

7304. No embalmer shall embalm a dead body without obtaining written or oral permission of a person who has the right to control the disposition of the remains pursuant to Section 7100, except that prior authorization is not required if embalming is necessary in order to comply with applicable laws or regulations, or is necessary to avoid irreparable deterioration of the dead body, in which case, a good faith effort shall be made to obtain permission. (Added by Stats. 1978, Ch. 530.)

§ 1214. Authorization to Accept or Decline Embalming
(Cal. Admin. Code tit. 16, § 1214, 16 CA ADC § 1214)

Except as otherwise provided in Health and Safety Code section 7304, human remains shall not be embalmed without the express authorization of a person having the legal right to control disposition of the remains. Such authorization, to either accept or decline embalming, shall be secured by use of form 12-AUTH (rev. 11/14) prescribed by the bureau and made a part of this regulation.

CREMATION

Eastern Orthodox Christians do not traditionally cremate loved ones after passing. This goes against the teachings of the Church and is actually forbidden in most dioceses in the United States. We prefer to return them into the earth after passing for a restful, undisturbed sleep, until Christ comes again, when our bodies will be resurrected.

One reason Orthodox Christians prefer not to cremate the departed is because we venerate and admire the relics of the saints. We believe that the body is the temple of the Holy Spirit, "... do you not know that your body is the temple of the Holy Spirit who is in you, whom you have from God, and you are not your own" (1 Corinthians 6:19), and remain honorable even after death. Keeping the bodies of our loved ones intact after death honors their existence and the belief that all Orthodox Christians remain in communion with God even after their physical death.

Furthermore, ancient Christians saw cremation as an act of dishonor since pagan emperors tried to dishonor Christians by burning them. Pagans denied the Christian understanding of life everlasting and resurrection. Burning a body is also seen as a punishment in the Old Testament, "So whoever is pointed out, he shall be burned with fire along with whatever he has, because he transgressed the covenant of the Lord and brought lawlessness in Israel" Joshua 7:15.

For those that choose cremation, you can still have a viewing and some places offer viewing of the cremation as well. Once the cremation is complete, the ashes will be brought to the funeral home by a courier. When the funeral home receives the ashes, they will contact the Next-of-Kin and schedule pick-up. There are also different service options a family can do with ashes, for example, if the family still wishes to have a procession they can. If your funeral home does not have the means to transport ashes in their hearse, contact someone who can. There are arks that urns are placed in, for protection, then are placed in the hearse just like a casket would.

We all have God given free will, but it is important for the Orthodox Christian to understand the stance on cremation in the Church. There are also cultural differences around the world, some countries may not have the space for an actual burial. Orthodox Christians should speak with their Priest on this matter.

ACKNOWLEDGEMENTS/ RESOURCES

California Cemetery and Funeral Bureau
https://www.cfb.ca.gov/laws_regs/existing_laws.shtml

The Orthodox Study Bible 2008

FTC- Federal Trade Commission – Funeral Rule

"Guidelines for Christian Burial", SS. Peter and Paul Orthodox
Church, Manville, NJ

www.ingramcontent.com/pod-product-compliance
Lightning Source LLC
Chambersburg PA
CBHW021812150726
47989CB00004B/1904